The Weekly Steps of
of
Life-long Love

A 16-month Engagement Diary

Activinotes

Activinotes
DAILY JOURNALS, PLANNERS, NOTEBOOKS AND OTHER BLANK BOOKS

Copyright 2016

Weekly Journal

_____
_____
_____
_____
_____
_____
_____
_____
_____
_____

notes:

_____
_____
_____
_____
_____
_____

_____
_____
_____

Month - 1

wedding preparation for this month

Weekly Journal

_____

_____

_____

_____

_____

_____

_____

_____

_____

_____

_____

_____

notes :

_____

_____

_____

_____

_____

_____

_____

_____

_____

_____

Weekly Journal

_____

_____

_____

_____

_____

_____

_____

_____

_____

_____

notes:

_____

_____

_____

_____

_____

_____

_____

_____

Weekly Journal

_____
_____
_____
_____
_____
_____
_____
_____
_____
_____

notes:

_____   _____
_____   _____
_____   _____
_____
_____
_____

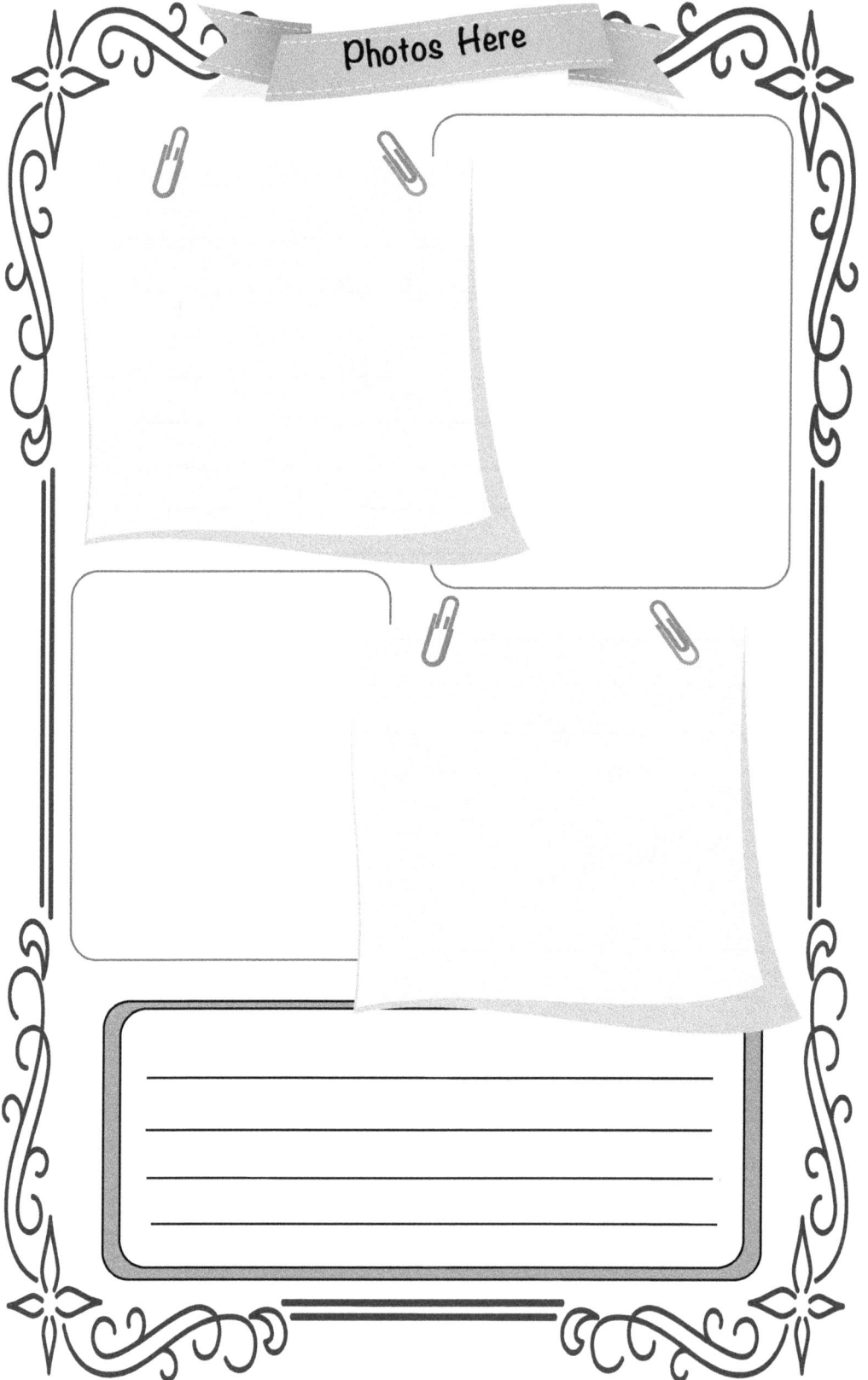

Photos Here

Month - 2

wedding preparation for this month

Weekly Journal

_____
_____
_____
_____
_____
_____
_____
_____
_____
_____
_____

NOTES :

_____

_____

_____

_____

_____

_____

_____

_____

_____

Weekly Journal

_____

_____

_____

_____

_____

_____

_____

_____

_____

_____

_____

notes :

_____   _____

_____   _____

_____   _____

_____

_____

_____

_____

Weekly Journal

notes :

Weekly Journal

_____
_____
_____
_____
_____
_____
_____
_____
_____
_____
_____
_____

notes:

_____   _____
_____   _____
_____   _____
_____   _____
_____
_____

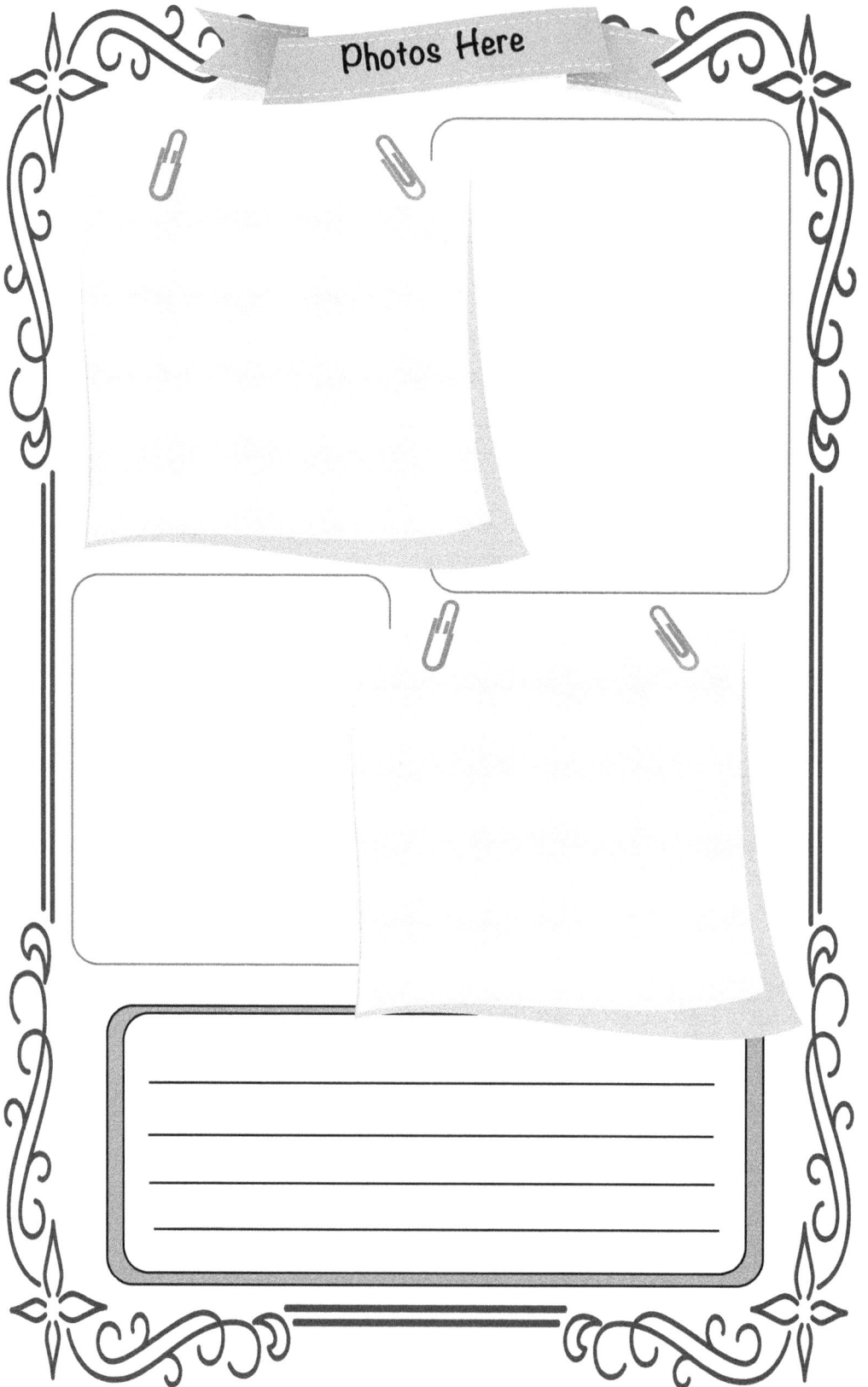

Photos Here

Month - 3

wedding preparation for this month

Weekly Journal

_____
_____
_____
_____
_____
_____
_____
_____
_____
_____
_____

notes:

_____   _____

_____   _____

_____   _____

_____

_____

_____

Weekly Journal

_____
_____
_____
_____
_____
_____
_____
_____
_____
_____
_____

notes:

_____

_____

_____

_____

_____

_____

_____

_____

Weekly Journal

_____
_____
_____
_____
_____
_____
_____
_____
_____
_____

notes:

_____   _____
_____   _____
_____   _____
_____
_____
_____
_____

Weekly Journal

_____
_____
_____
_____
_____
_____
_____
_____
_____
_____

notes :

_____
_____
_____
_____
_____

_____
_____
_____
_____

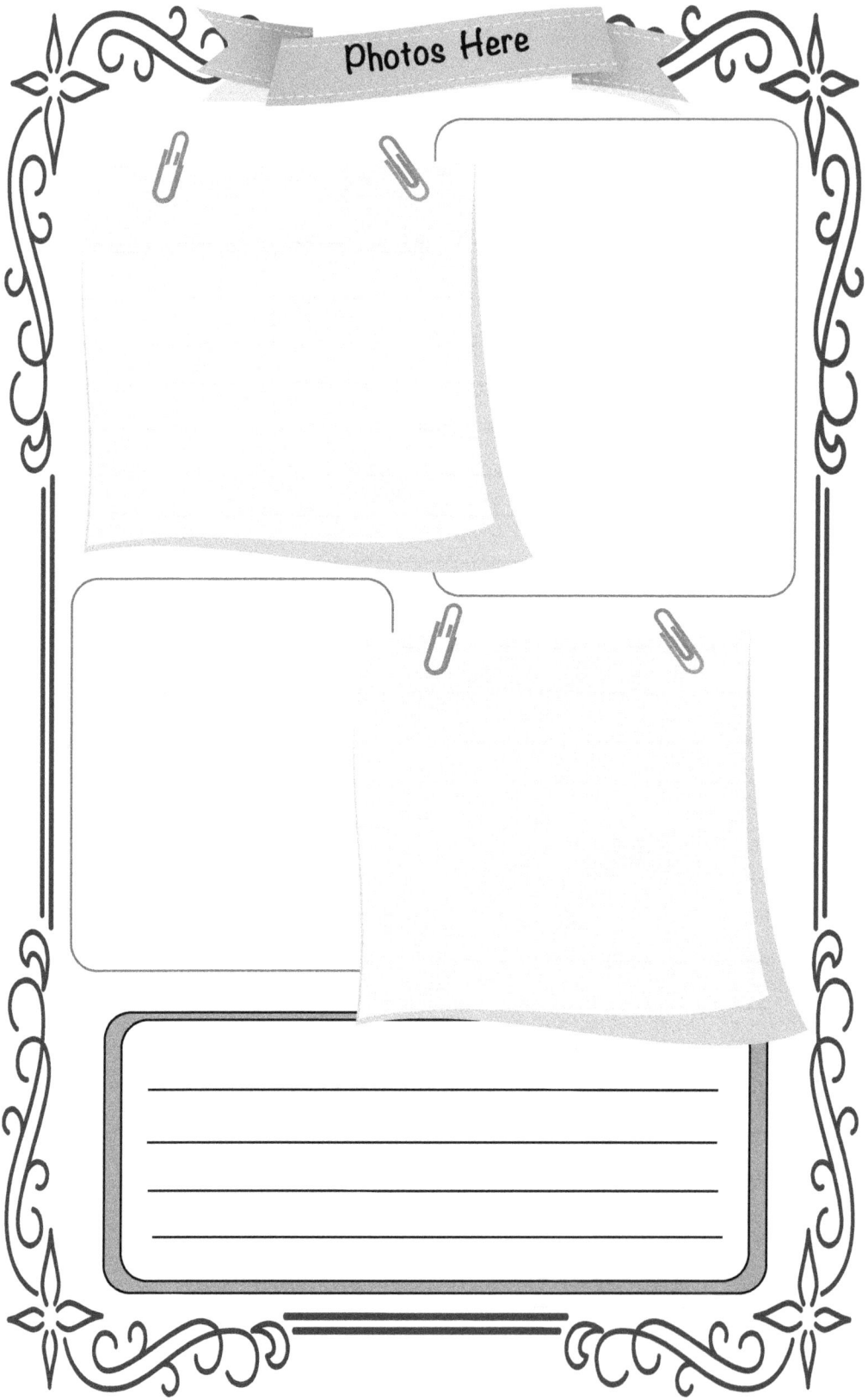

Photos Here

Month - 4

wedding preparation for this month

Weekly Journal

_____
_____
_____
_____
_____
_____
_____
_____
_____
_____

notes:

_____
_____

_____
_____
_____
_____
_____
_____

Weekly Journal

_____
_____
_____
_____
_____
_____
_____
_____
_____
_____
_____

notes:

_____
_____
_____
_____

_____
_____
_____
_____
_____
_____
_____

Weekly Journal

_____
_____
_____
_____
_____
_____
_____
_____
_____
_____
_____

notes:

_____
_____
_____
_____
_____
_____

_____
_____
_____
_____

Weekly Journal

---

notes:

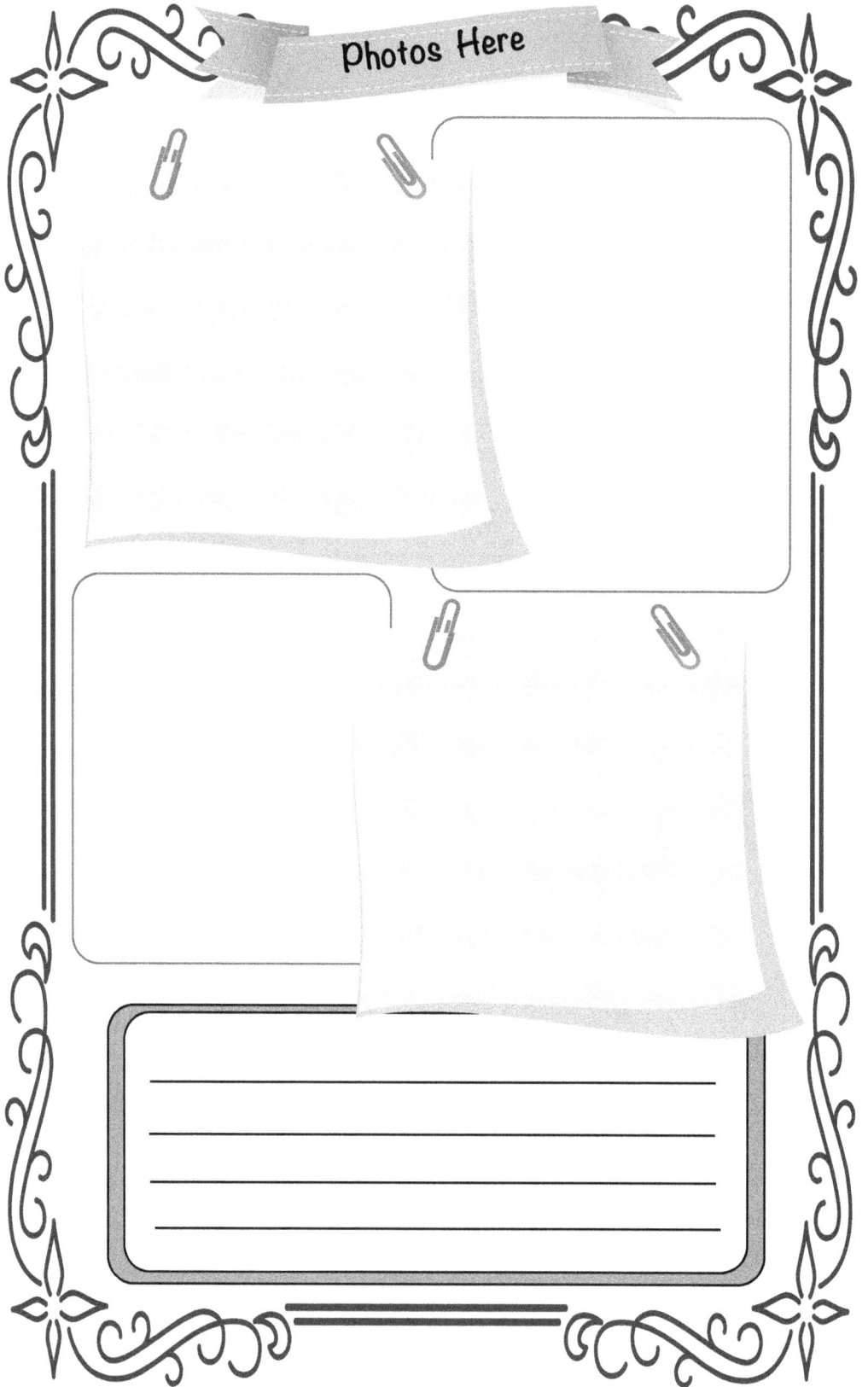

Month - 5

wedding preparation for this month

Weekly Journal

_____
_____
_____
_____
_____
_____
_____
_____
_____
_____
_____

notes:

_____
_____
_____

_____
_____
_____
_____

Weekly Journal

_____
_____
_____
_____
_____
_____
_____
_____
_____
_____
_____

notes:

_____
_____
_____
_____
_____
_____

_____
_____
_____
_____

Weekly Journal

_____
_____
_____
_____
_____
_____
_____
_____
_____
_____
_____

notes :

_____

_____

_____

_____

_____

_____

_____

Weekly Journal

_____

_____

_____

_____

_____

_____

_____

_____

_____

notes:

_____

_____

_____

_____

_____

_____

_____

_____

Month - 6

wedding preparation for this month

Weekly Journal

_____
_____
_____
_____
_____
_____
_____
_____
_____

notes :

_____   _____
                                         _____
_____   _____
_____
_____
_____
_____
_____

Weekly Journal

_____

_____

_____

_____

_____

_____

_____

_____

_____

_____

_____

notes :

_____   _____

_____   _____

_____   _____

_____

_____

_____

_____

Weekly Journal

_____
_____
_____
_____
_____
_____
_____
_____
_____
_____
_____

notes:

_____   _____
_____   _____
_____   _____
_____   _____
_____
_____
_____
_____

Weekly Journal

_____

_____

_____

_____

_____

_____

_____

_____

_____

_____

_____

_____

notes:

_____

_____

_____

_____

_____

_____

_____

_____

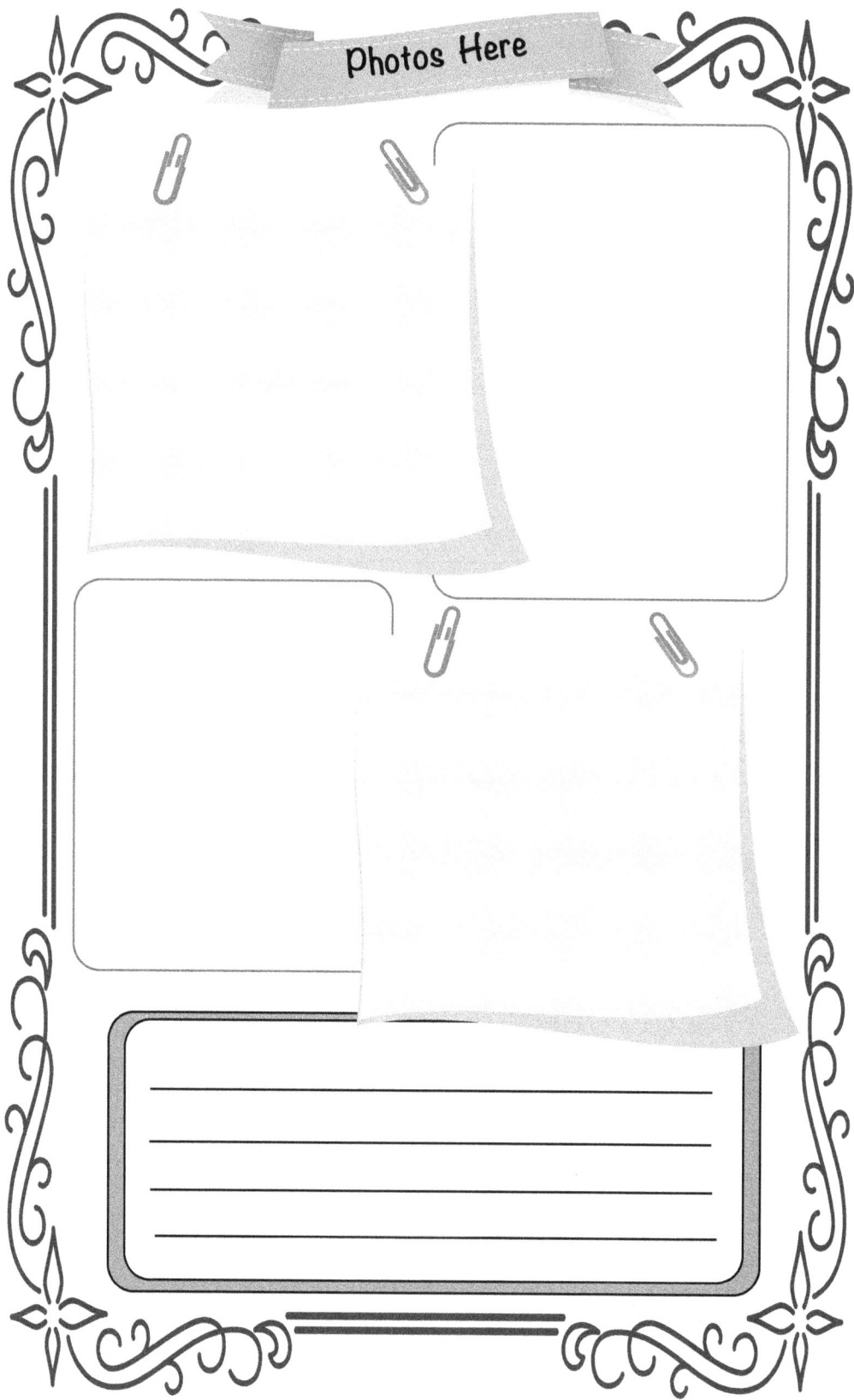

Photos Here

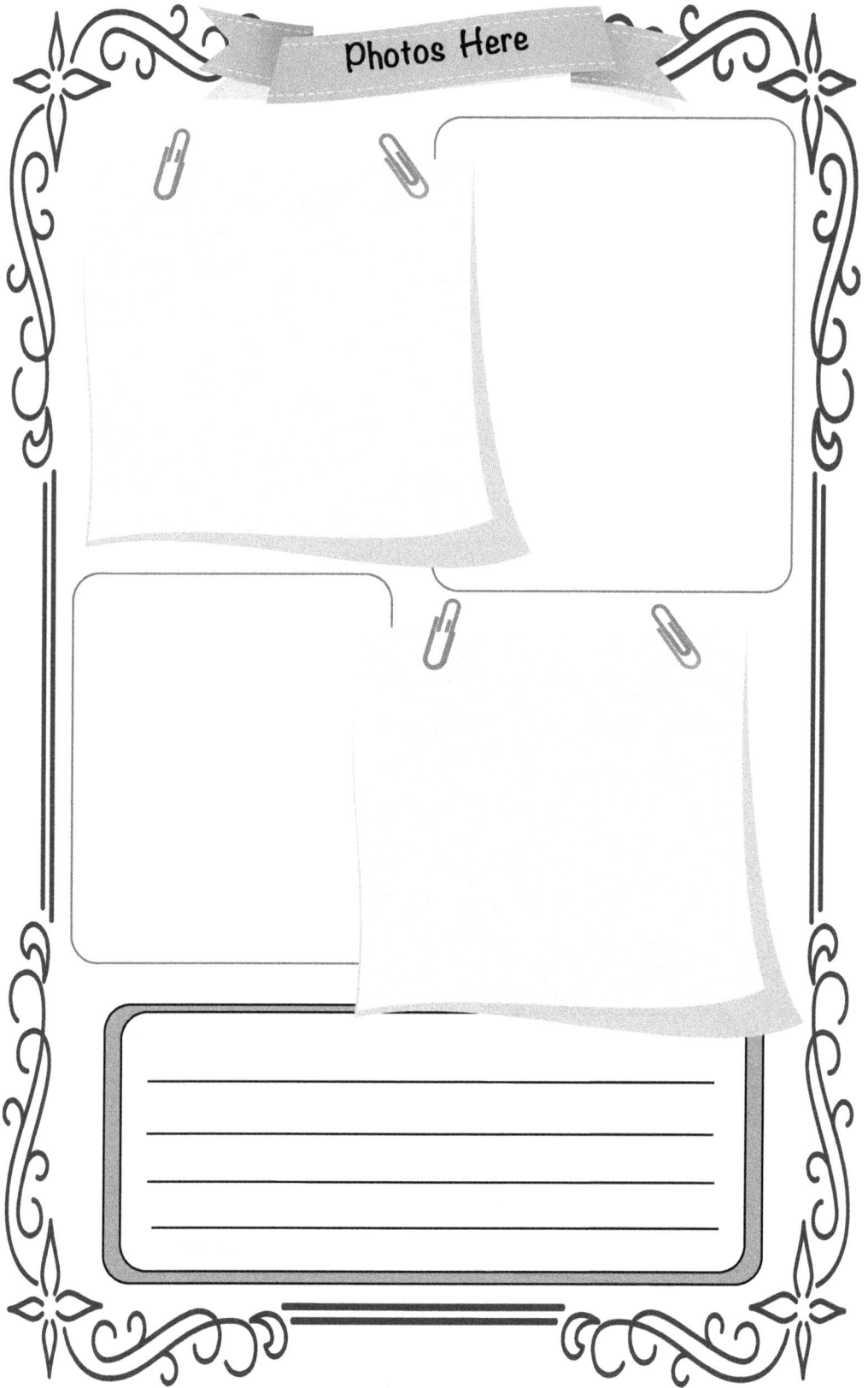

Month - 7

wedding preparation for this month

Weekly Journal

_____

_____

_____

_____

_____

_____

_____

_____

_____

_____

_____

notes:

_____   _____

_____   _____

_____   _____

_____   _____

_____

_____

_____

_____

Weekly Journal

_____
_____
_____
_____
_____
_____
_____
_____
_____
_____
_____
_____

notes :

_____
_____
_____
_____
_____
_____
_____
_____

Weekly Journal

_____

_____

_____

_____

_____

_____

_____

_____

_____

_____

_____

notes:

_____

_____

_____

_____

_____

_____

_____

_____

Weekly Journal

_____
_____
_____
_____
_____
_____
_____
_____
_____
_____
_____

notes:

_____   _____
_____   _____
_____   _____
_____   _____
_____
_____

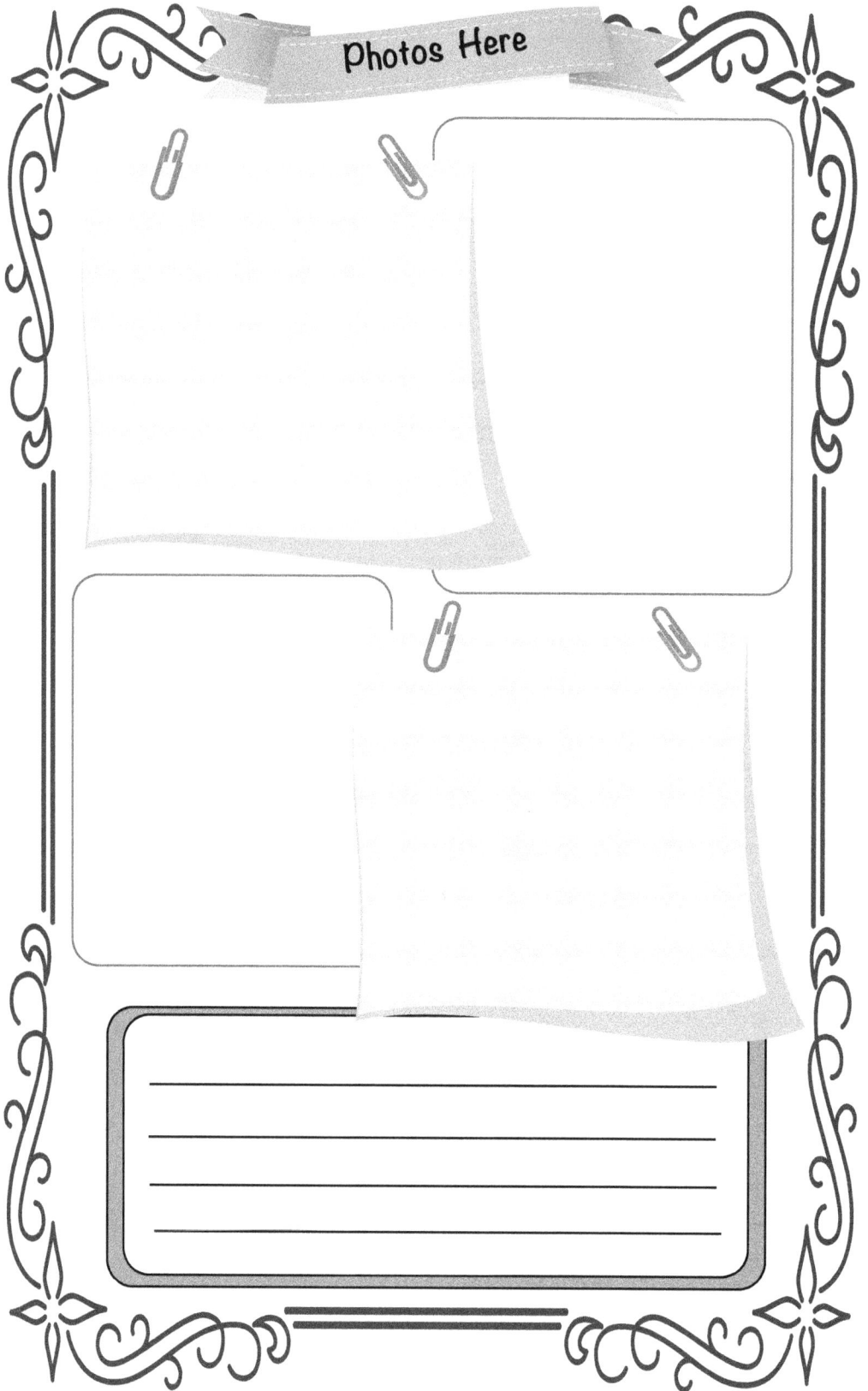

Photos Here

Month - 8

wedding preparation for this month

Weekly Journal

_____
_____
_____
_____
_____
_____
_____
_____
_____
_____
_____
_____

Notes:

_____
_____
_____
_____
_____
_____
_____

Weekly Journal

_____
_____
_____
_____
_____
_____
_____
_____
_____
_____

notes:

_____
_____
_____

_____
_____
_____
_____

Weekly Journal

_____

_____

_____

_____

_____

_____

_____

_____

_____

_____

_____

_____

notes:

_____

_____

_____

_____

_____

_____

_____

_____

_____

Weekly Journal

_____
_____
_____
_____
_____
_____
_____
_____
_____
_____

notes:

_____   _____
_____   _____
_____   _____
_____
_____
_____

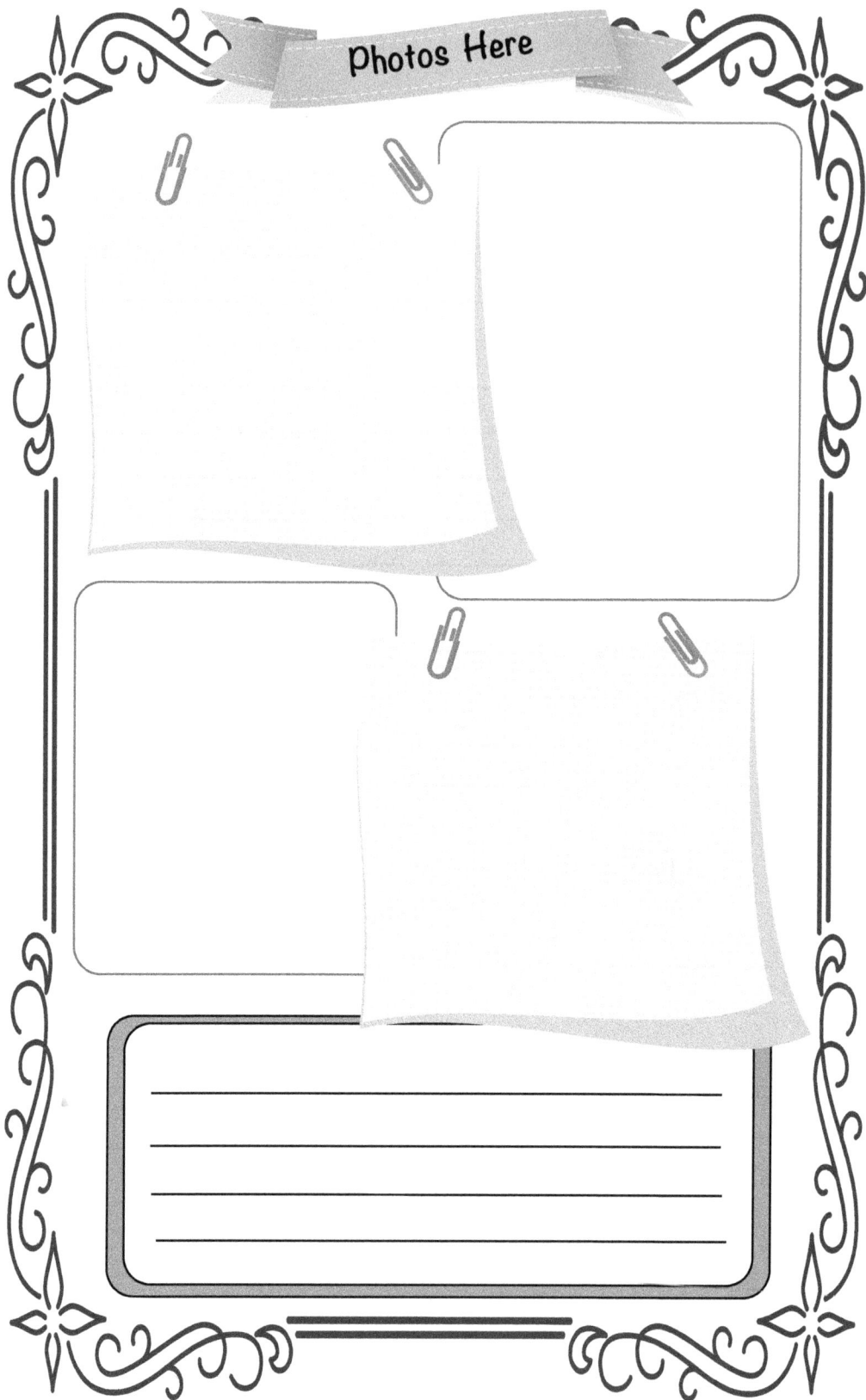

Photos Here

Month - 9

wedding preparation for this month

Weekly Journal

_____
_____
_____
_____
_____
_____
_____
_____
_____
_____

notes :

_____
_____
_____
_____
_____
_____

_____
_____
_____

Weekly Journal

_____
_____
_____
_____
_____
_____
_____
_____
_____
_____
_____

notes:

_____   _____
_____   _____
_____   _____
_____   _____
_____
_____
_____

Weekly Journal

_____

_____

_____

_____

_____

_____

_____

_____

_____

_____

_____

notes:

_____   _____

_____   _____

_____   _____

_____   _____

_____

_____

_____

Weekly Journal

_____
_____
_____
_____
_____
_____
_____
_____
_____
_____
_____

Notes:

_____   _____
_____   _____
_____   _____
_____   _____
_____
_____
_____

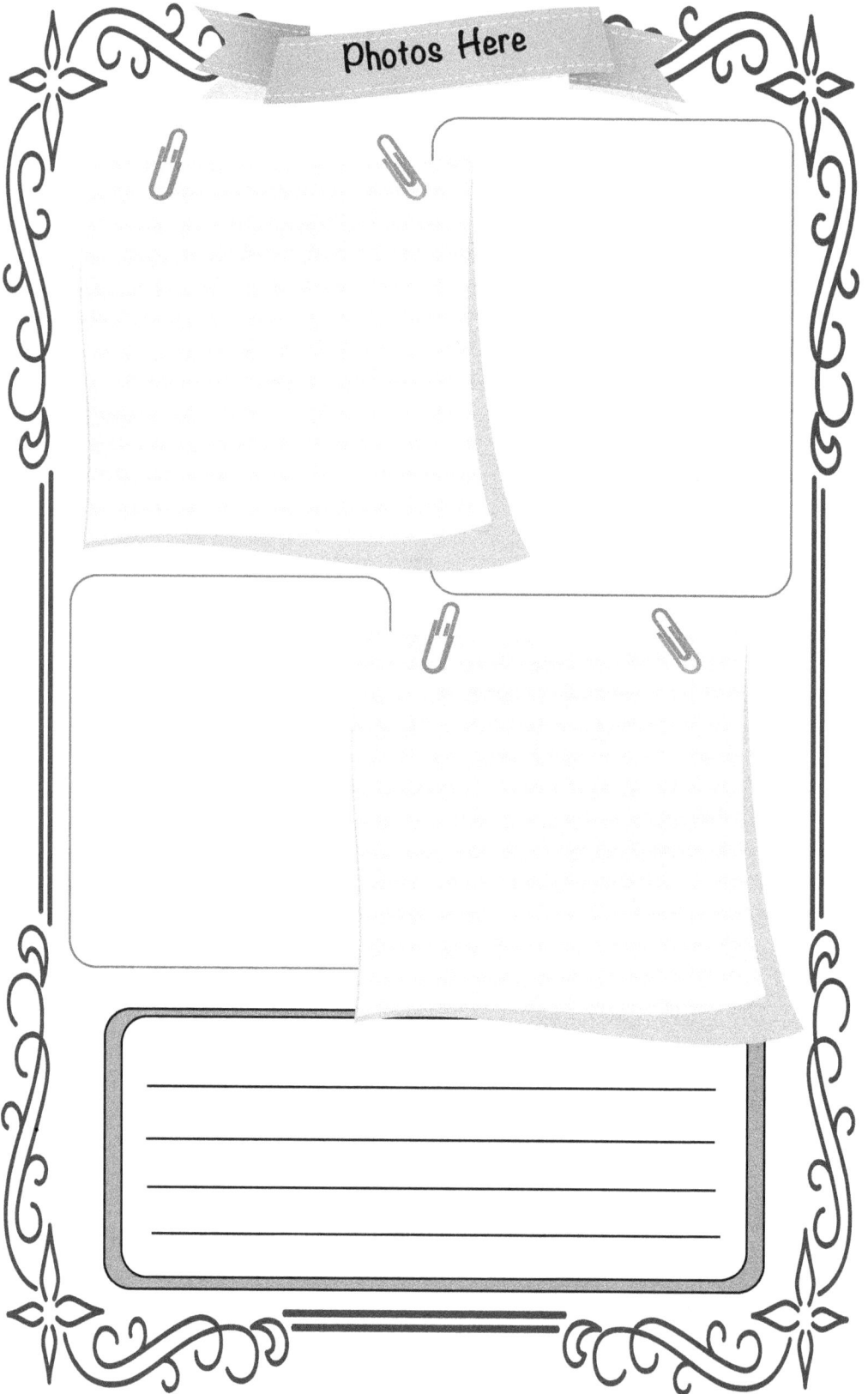

Photos Here

Month - 10

wedding preparation for this month

Weekly Journal

_____
_____
_____
_____
_____
_____
_____
_____
_____
_____
_____
_____

notes :

_____
_____

_____
_____
_____
_____
_____
_____

Weekly Journal

_____

_____

_____

_____

_____

_____

_____

_____

_____

_____

NOTES:

_____

_____

_____

_____

_____

_____

_____

_____

Weekly Journal

_____

_____

_____

_____

_____

_____

_____

_____

_____

_____

notes :

_____

_____

_____

_____

_____

_____

_____

_____

_____

Weekly Journal

_____

_____

_____

_____

_____

_____

_____

_____

_____

_____

_____

notes:

_____   _____

_____   _____

_____   _____

_____

_____

_____

_____

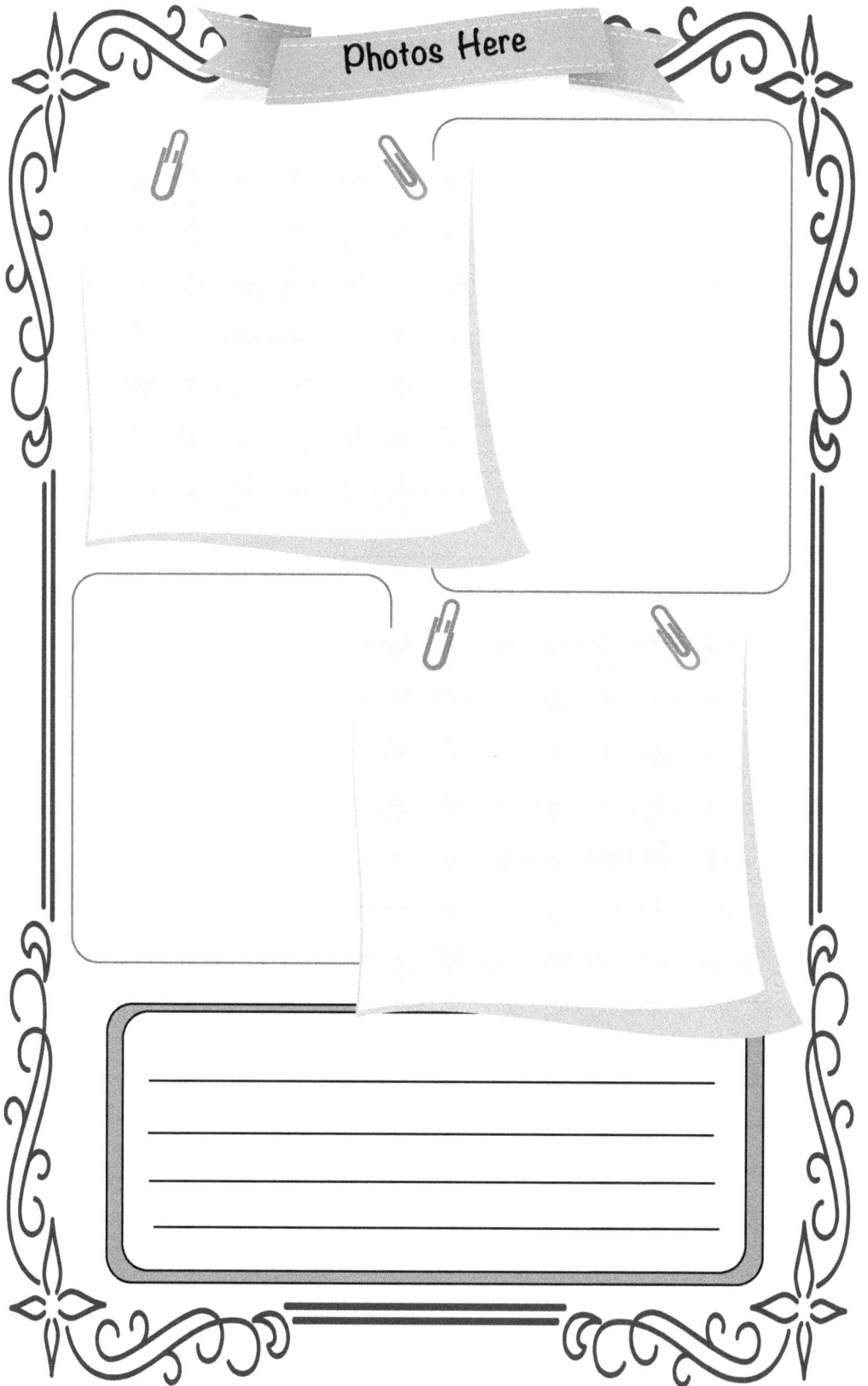

Month - 11

wedding preparation for this month

Weekly Journal

_____
_____
_____
_____
_____
_____
_____
_____
_____
_____

notes :

_____

_____

_____

_____

_____

_____

_____

Weekly Journal

_____

_____

_____

_____

_____

_____

_____

_____

_____

_____

notes:

_____   _____

_____   _____

_____   _____

_____   _____

_____

_____

_____

Weekly Journal

notes :

Weekly Journal

_____
_____
_____
_____
_____
_____
_____
_____
_____
_____

NOTES:

_____   _____
_____   _____
_____   _____
_____
_____
_____

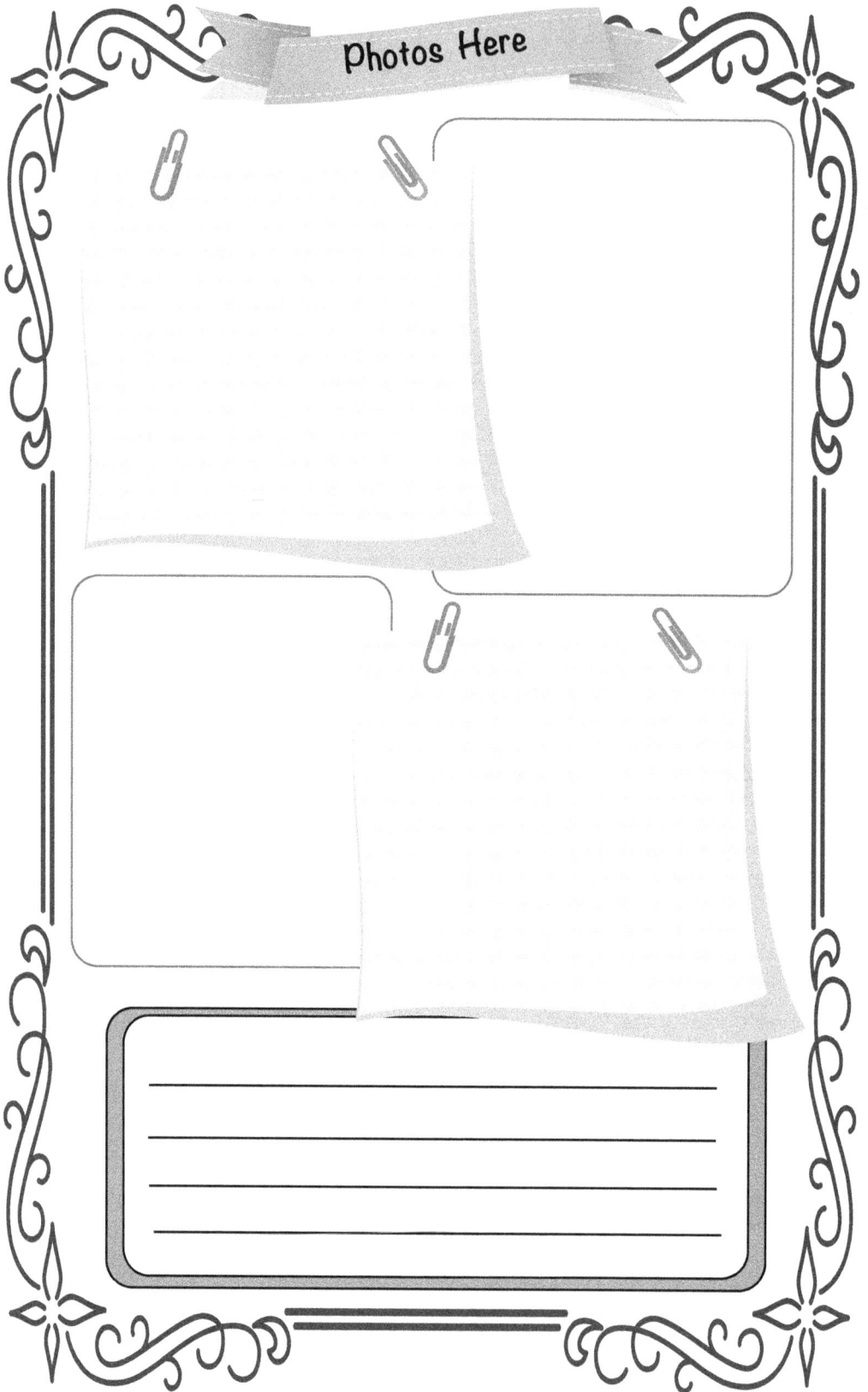

Month - 12

wedding preparation for this month

Weekly Journal

_____
_____
_____
_____
_____
_____
_____
_____
_____
_____
_____

notes:

_____
_____
_____
_____
_____
_____
_____
_____

Weekly Journal

_____
_____
_____
_____
_____
_____
_____
_____
_____
_____
_____

notes:

_____   _____
_____   _____
_____   _____
_____   _____
_____
_____

Weekly Journal

_____
_____
_____
_____
_____
_____
_____
_____
_____
_____
_____

notes :

_____
_____
_____
_____
_____
_____

Weekly Journal

_____

_____

_____

_____

_____

_____

_____

_____

_____

_____

_____

notes:

_____

_____

_____

_____

_____

_____

_____

_____

_____

_____

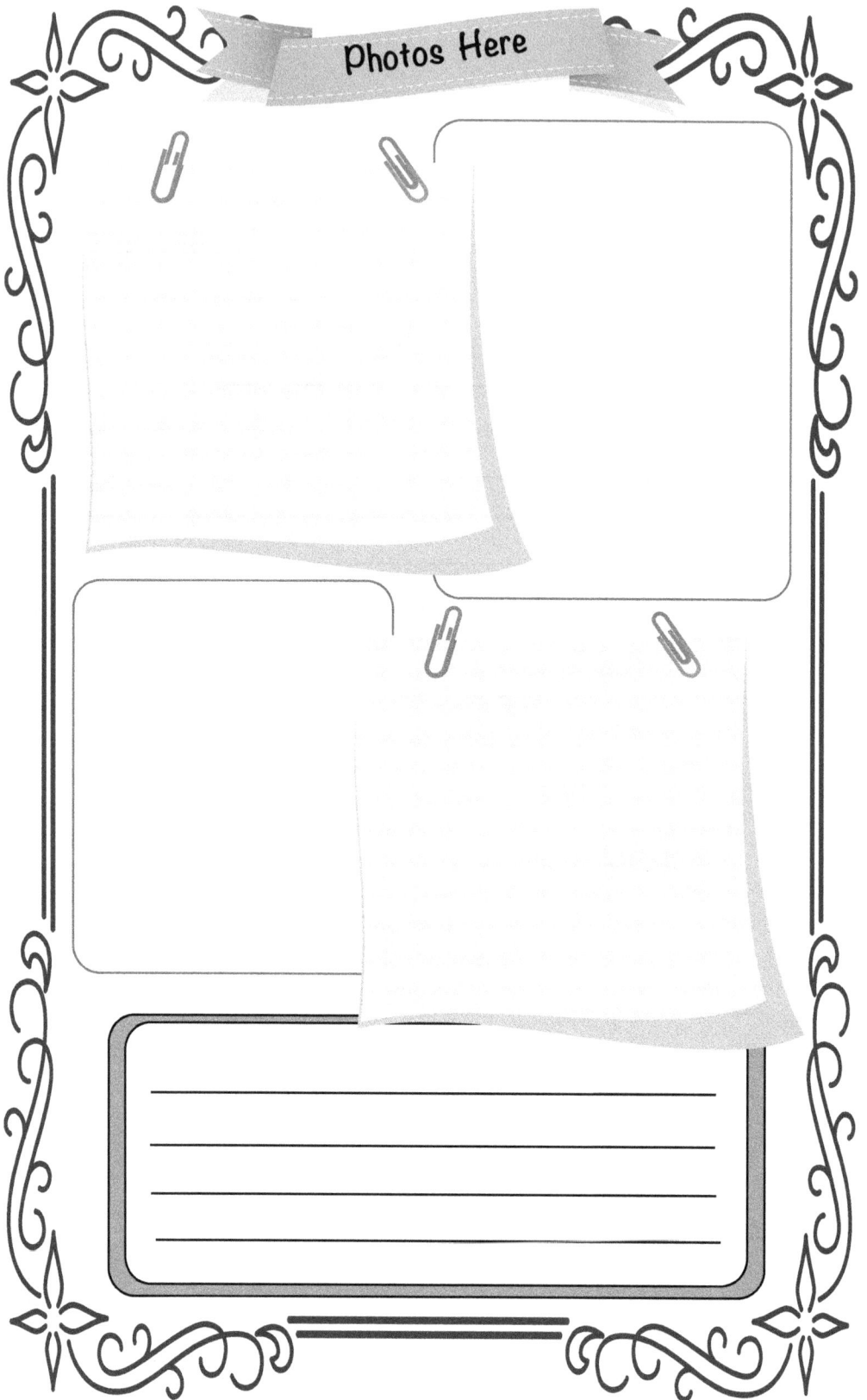

Photos Here

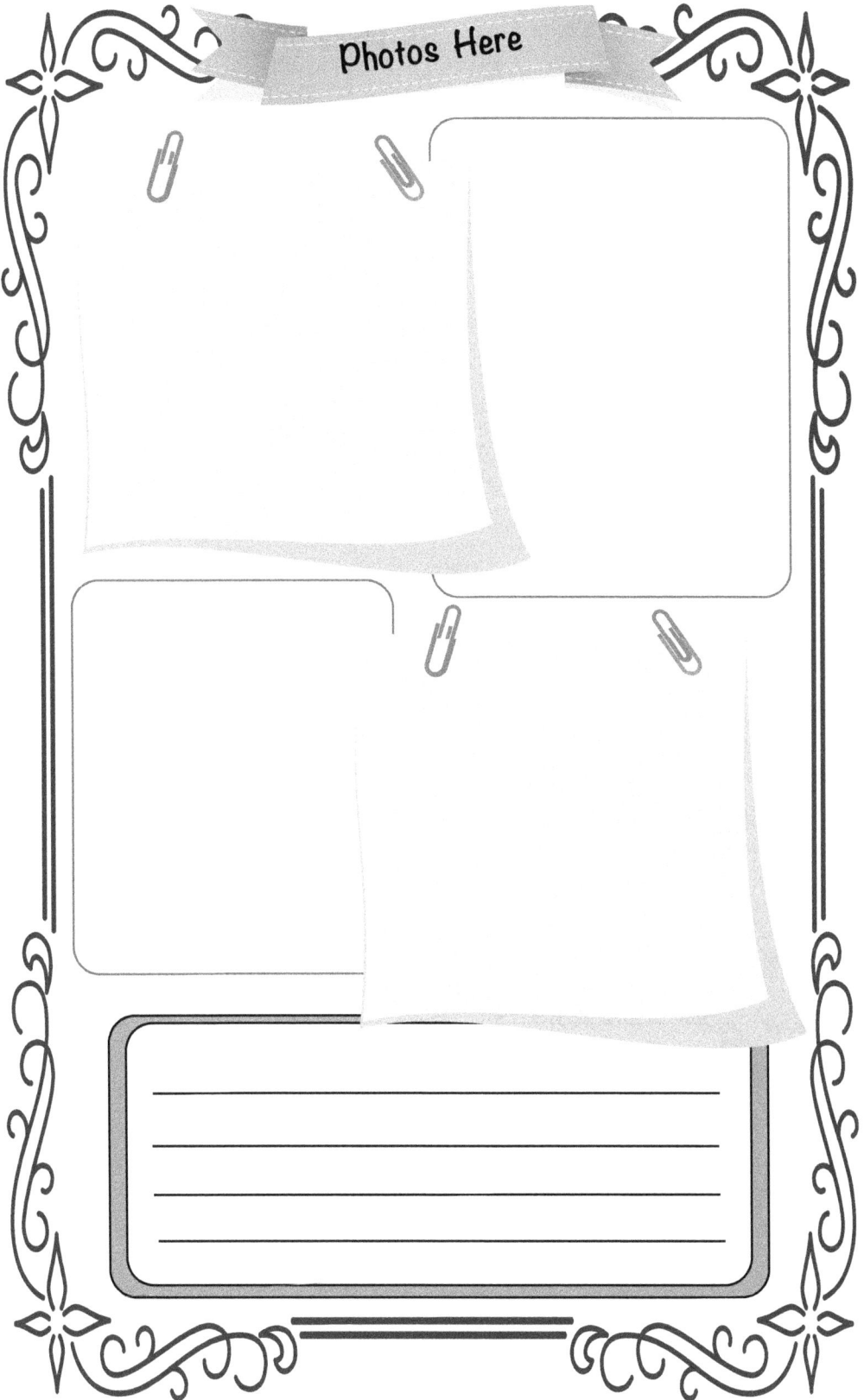

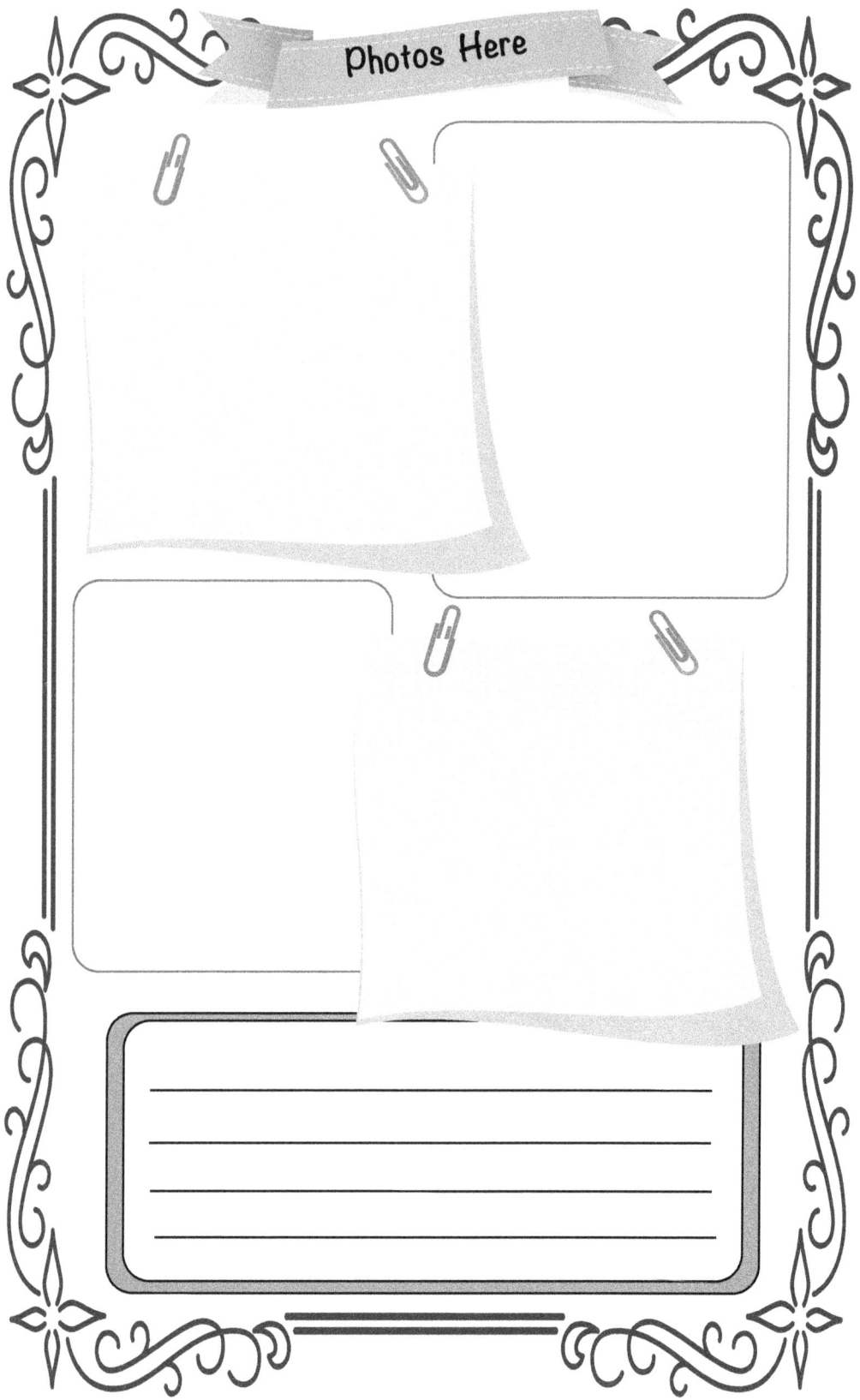

Month - 13

wedding preparation for this month

Weekly Journal

_____

_____

_____

_____

_____

_____

_____

_____

_____

_____

_____

NOTES:

_____

_____

_____

_____

_____

_____

_____

Weekly Journal

_____

_____

_____

_____

_____

_____

_____

_____

_____

_____

notes:

_____

_____

_____

_____

_____

_____

_____

_____

_____

Weekly Journal

_____

_____

_____

_____

_____

_____

_____

_____

_____

_____

_____

notes :

_____

_____

_____

_____

_____

_____

_____

_____

_____

Weekly Journal

_____
_____
_____
_____
_____
_____
_____
_____
_____
_____

notes :

_____   _____
_____   _____
_____   _____
_____   _____
_____
_____
_____
_____

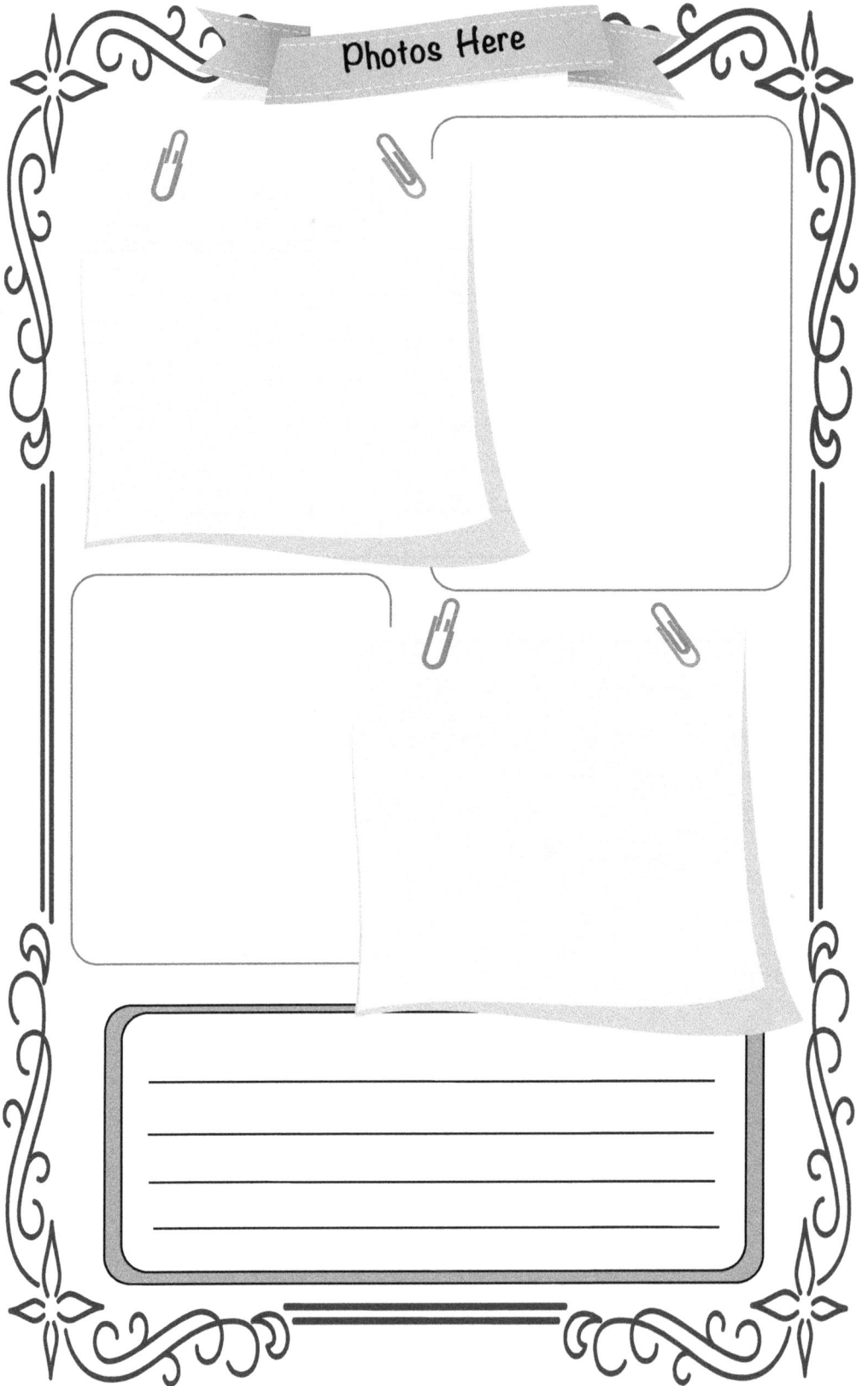

Month - 14

wedding preparation for this month

Weekly Journal

_____
_____
_____
_____
_____
_____
_____
_____
_____
_____

notes :

_____
_____
_____
_____
_____
_____

Weekly Journal

_____
_____
_____
_____
_____
_____
_____
_____
_____
_____

notes:

_____

_____
_____
_____
_____
_____

Weekly Journal

_____
_____
_____
_____
_____
_____
_____
_____
_____
_____
_____

notes:

_____

_____
_____
_____

_____
_____
_____
_____

Weekly Journal

_____
_____
_____
_____
_____
_____
_____
_____
_____
_____

notes:

_____   _____
_____   _____
_____   _____
_____
_____
_____
_____

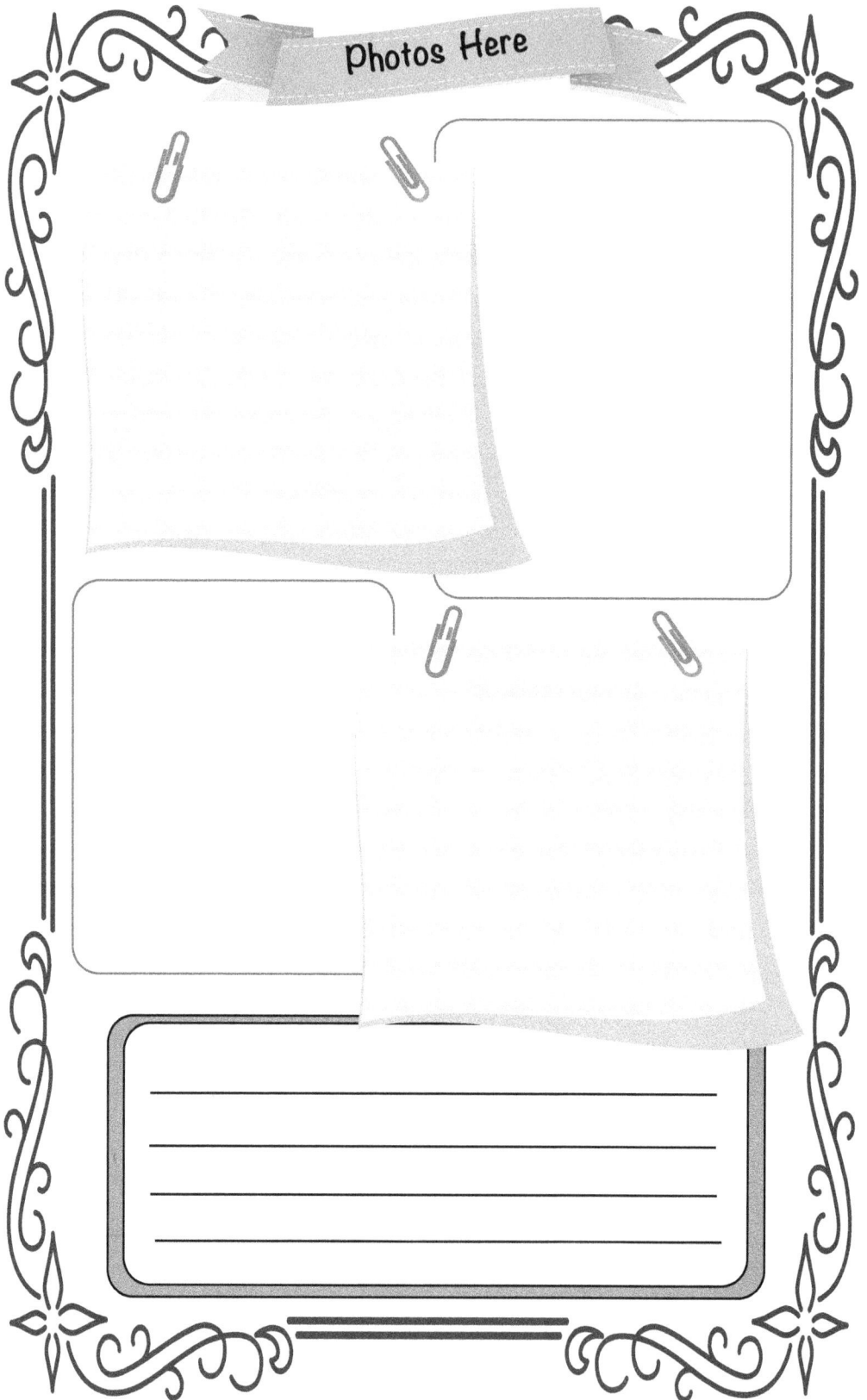

Month - 15

wedding preparation for this month

Weekly Journal

_____
_____
_____
_____
_____
_____
_____
_____
_____
_____
_____

notes:

_____
_____
_____
_____
_____
_____

Weekly Journal

_____

_____

_____

_____

_____

_____

_____

_____

_____

_____

_____

notes :

_____

_____

_____

_____

_____

_____

_____

_____

_____

Weekly Journal

_____
_____
_____
_____
_____
_____
_____
_____
_____

notes :

_____

_____

_____

_____

_____

_____

_____

Weekly Journal

_____

_____

_____

_____

_____

_____

_____

_____

_____

notes :

_____

_____

_____

_____

_____

_____

_____

_____

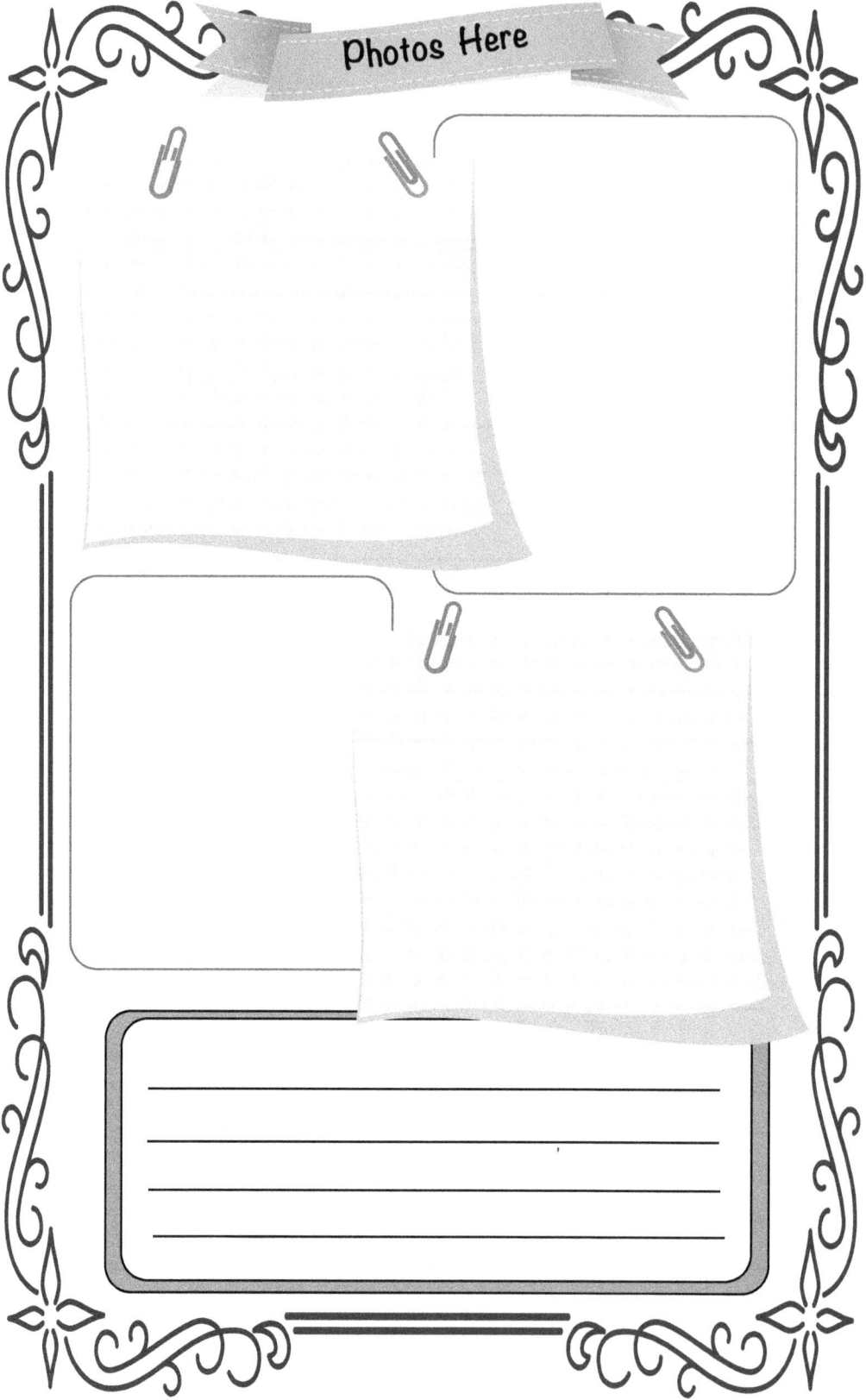

Photos Here

Month - 16

wedding preparation for this month

Weekly Journal

_____
_____
_____
_____
_____
_____
_____
_____
_____
_____
_____

notes:

_____   _____
_____   _____
_____   _____
_____   _____
_____
_____
_____

Weekly Journal

_____
_____
_____
_____
_____
_____
_____
_____
_____
_____
_____

notes:

_____   _____
_____   _____
_____   _____
_____   _____
_____
_____

Weekly Journal

_____
_____
_____
_____
_____
_____
_____
_____
_____
_____
_____
_____

notes:

_____
_____

_____
_____
_____
_____
_____

Weekly Journal

_____
_____
_____
_____
_____
_____
_____
_____
_____
_____

notes:

_____
_____
_____
_____
_____
_____
_____

_____
_____
_____
_____

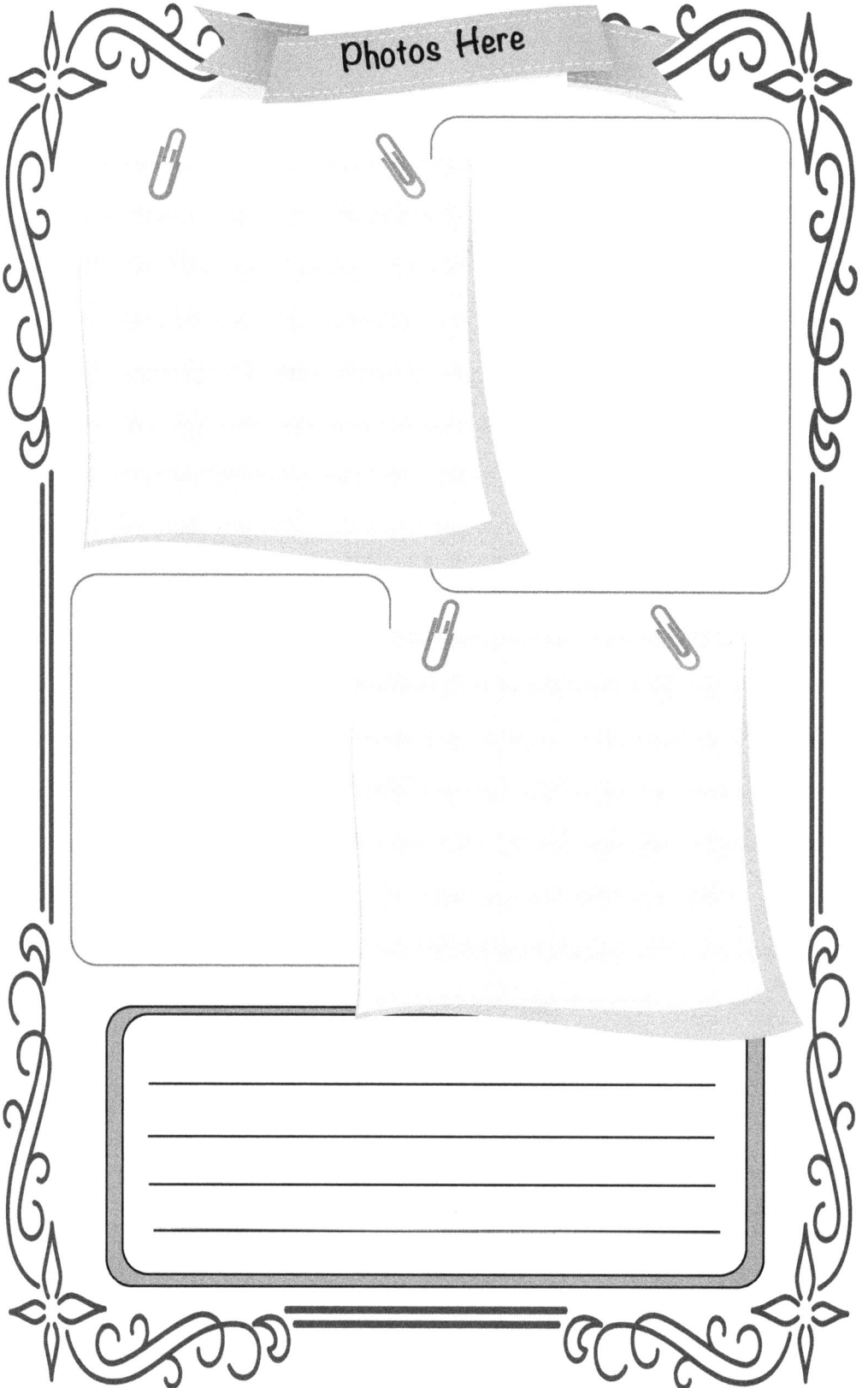

Photos Here

More Photos here

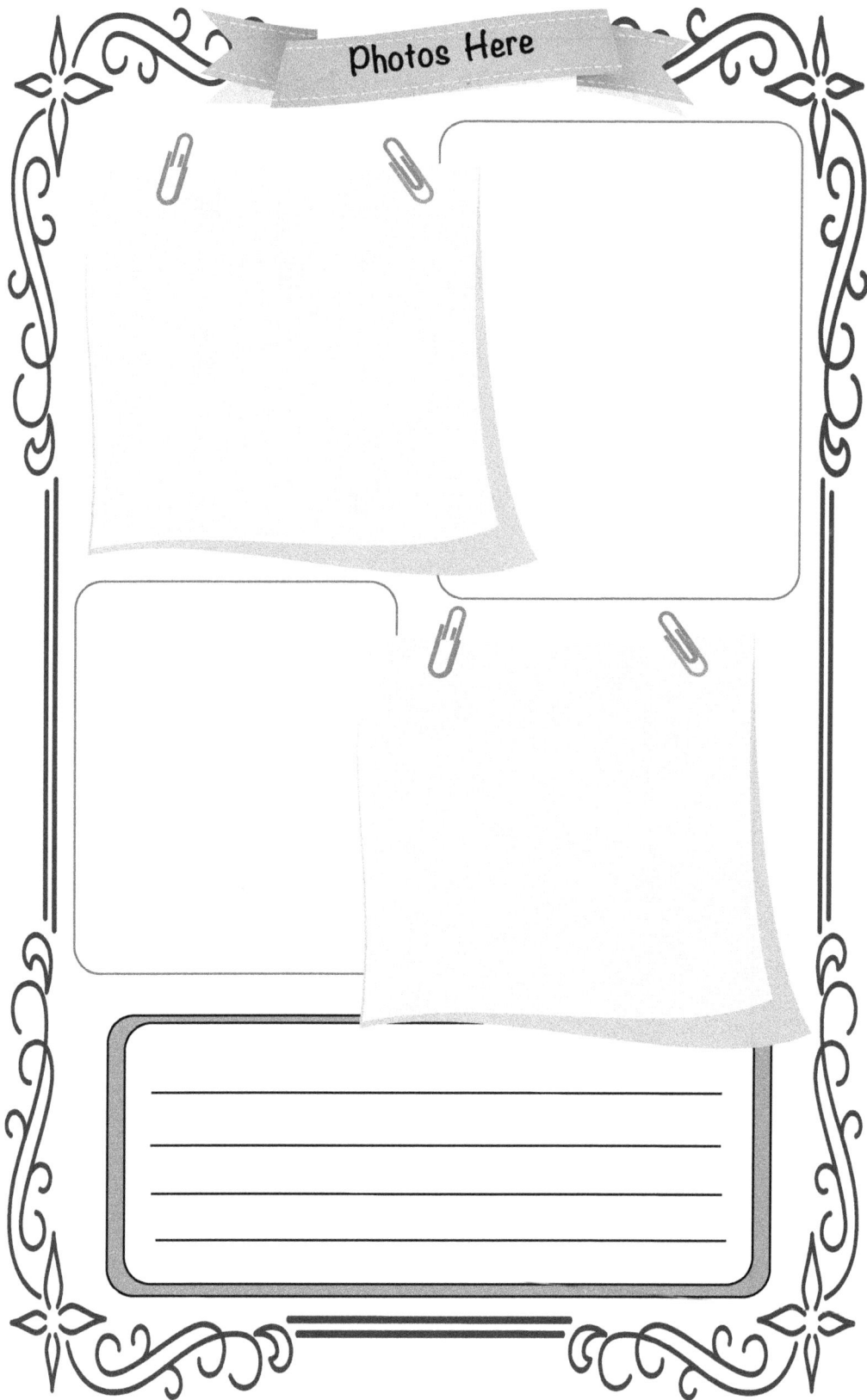

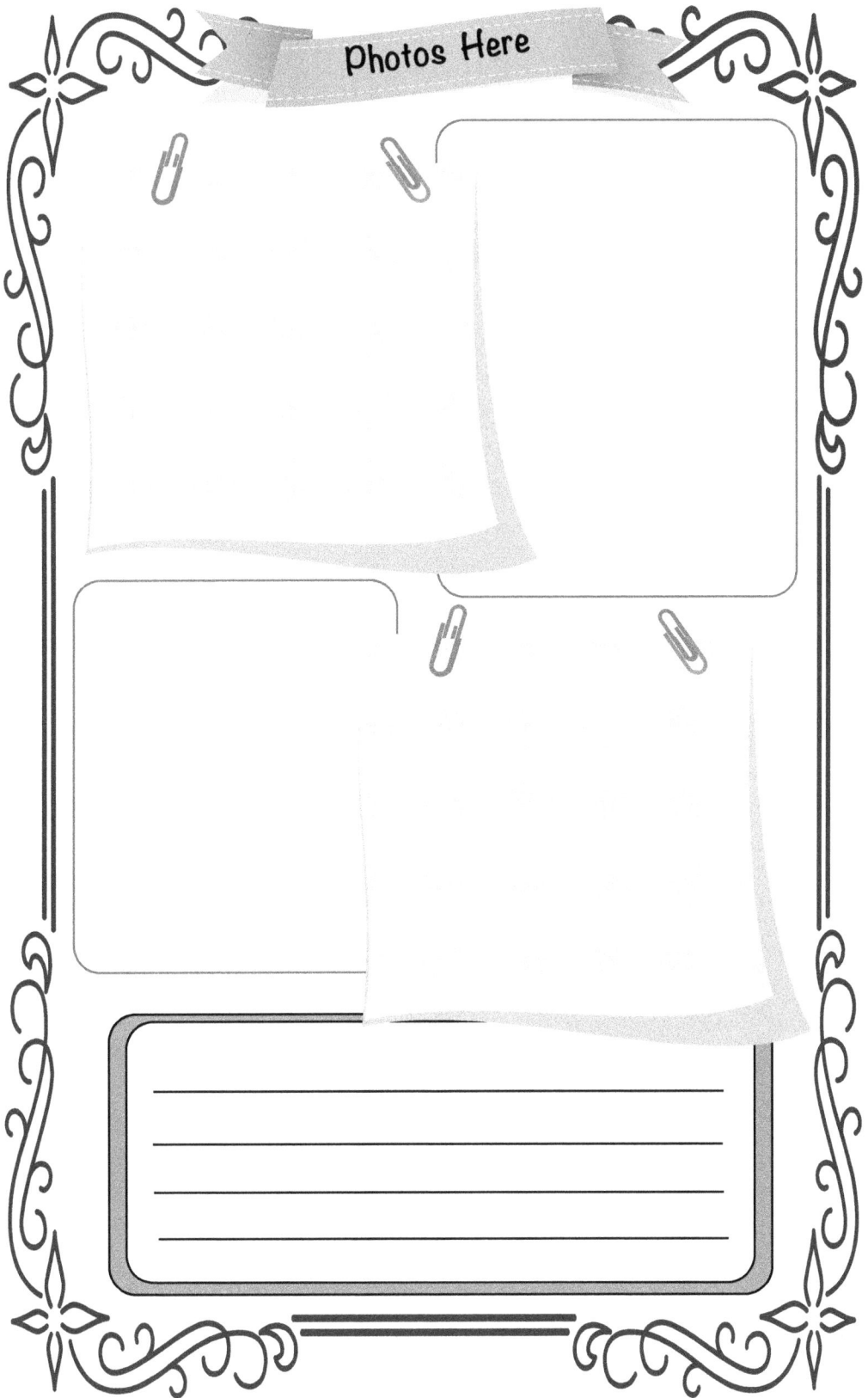

Photos Here

www.ingramcontent.com/pod-product-compliance
Lightning Source LLC
Chambersburg PA
CBHW081338090426
42737CB00017B/3195